SENTENCES AND RAIN

OTHER BOOKS BY ELAINE EQUI

Click and Clone, 2011

Ripple Effect: New & Selected Poems, 2007

The Cloud of Knowable Things, 2003

Voice-Over, 1998

Friendship with Things, 1998

Decoy, 1994

Surface Tension, 1989

Views without Rooms, 1989

Accessories, 1988

The Corners of the Mouth, 1986

Shrewcrazy, 1981

Federal Woman, 1978

SENTENCES AND RAIN

ELAINE EQUI

COFFEE HOUSE PRESS
MINNEAPOLIS
2015

COVER DESIGN by Linda Koutsky
COVER ART © Eve Aschheim, "Streak/shift," from the Louis-Dreyfus Family Collection, photographed by Christopher Burke Studios
BOOK DESIGN by Connie Kuhnz
AUTHOR PHOTO © Becket Logan

Coffee House Press books are available to the trade through our primary distributor, Consortium Book Sales & Distribution, cbsd.com or (800) 283-3572. For personal orders, catalogs, or other information, write to: info@coffeehousepress.org. Coffee House Press is a nonprofit literary publishing house. Support from private foundations, corporate giving programs, government programs, and generous individuals helps make the publication of our books possible. We gratefully acknowledge their support in detail in the back of this book. Visit us at coffeehousepress.org.

LIBRARY OF CONGRESS
CATALOGING-IN-PUBLICATION DATA

Equi, Elaine.
[Poems. Selections]
Sentences and rain / Elaine Equi.
pages ; cm
ISBN 978-1-56689-421-0 (softcover)
I. Title.
PS3555.Q5A6 2015
811'.54—DC23

PRINTED IN THE UNITED STATES

FIRST EDITION | FIRST PRINTING

ACKNOWLEDGMENTS

Thanks to the editors of the following magazines, where some of these poems first appeared: the *American Poetry Review, Ampersand Review, Black Tongue Review, Caliban, Columbia Poetry Review, Court Green, Evergreen Review, Harvard Review, Lo-Ball, Mad Hat Review, Maggy, New American Writing, Ping Pong, Plume, Port, Posit, Right Hand Pointing, Stare, Talisman, Vanitas,* and *Volt*. "A Story Begins" was included in *The Best American Poetry* 2012, edited by Mark Doty and David Lehman.

Sixteen of these poems were also published as a chapbook entitled *Cut to the Chase*, with drawings by Geoffrey Young (Glory of Love Press, 2013).

for Allan Kornblum
with eternal gratitude and a double espresso

Contents

Spontaneous Generation

Luminous flank
cut from darkness —

floating free
as a new century

where the young
are implacable

and the old are crazy
and do as they please.

How did a silent movie
give birth to a nation?

How did a mouse, a shirt,
and a few grains

of wheat grow up
to be the president?

Cardboard Figures in a Landscape

A truck goes by.

It sounds like a truck

full of boxes.
Heavy things

getting jostled,
sliding around

on top of each other.
Sex between boxes.

With boxes
one doesn't know

what one is getting into.
A thud. A thump.

A loud horn
signals the climax,

satisfying for all.

In Black and White

X-ray of a day's
bones and teeth.

Blonde flowers,
black water,
shadows at play.

Hot jazz and cool jazz.

Dominoes and dice.

Spades and clubs,
but not diamonds or hearts
unless gray diamonds, gray hearts.

The inner silver being
that likes wandering
the inside-out underworld
of B movies,

and silent movies,
their quiet sister.

There is nothing so clean
and polished
or dirty as black and white.

Typography of the logos.

Original sin.

The Garden of Eden
was black and white,

the color added later.

If I Have Just One Word

Well, still that's a lot
of possibility.

A word can be a shriek
or a chrysanthemum —

barbed
or honeyed —

or maybe one of those
nonchalant, writerly words,

a preposition, pronoun,
conjunction on its way
to the soiree of a paragraph,

something to say
there's plenty more
where that came from.

The Dark Age of Summer

for John Ashbery

The days are long and dull and perilously bright
as I stroll the leafy corridor of the Academy.
Here, a near-nude body flexes his dumbbells.
There, a Samson upholds the twin pillars
of chocolate and vanilla ice cream.
No one but one has ever been outside
in the cool air and lived to tell the story
of our shadows parading before the garage door
with tongs and fly swatters. We have no memory
of times past — or an otherwise world, lush and verdant,
uncontaminated by ideas of any kind.

Umbrella Photo Poems

1.

The skinny arms.
The baggy shorts.

It's quite a surprise
to find an old man
reading the newspaper
under a peach silk parasol.

2.

My Cassandra's name
is Theodore.

She sits in the park
interpreting dreams for free
in order to pay
for mortuary school.

She's very knowledgeable
about such things.

If you wish to find her,
look for the rainbow-striped
umbrella that's always with her
like Joseph's coat of many colors
and say I sent you.

3.

An orange disc
out wandering
like a comet.

4.

There goes an enlightened beauty
with great posture.

Her umbrella is just the extension
of her slender body.

A halo of lime-green sky
springs from the correctness of her thoughts
and follows her around.

It comes complete with its own bluebirds.

Sentences and Rain

The rain
        waters
                the sentences.

The words
        grow taller,
                more supple.

The sentences
        previously
                too dry

now bend
        and reach
                toward meaning.

Like us they thirst
        for liquid cadence.
                As the rain reigns

all morning
        and afternoon,
                its lullaby

hushes the sentences,
        allows the words
                to drench us all at once.

Royal Feathers

Rakish pheasants
reeking of autumn.

~

Snowy
Pegasus
preening.

~

The owl
of Minerva's
speckled coat.

~

Raphael's resplendent
green-gilded
wave of wing.

~

Flannery O'Connor's
slow and lazy-eyed
peacock fan.

~

Garish showgirls
choked by
ostrich boas.

~

Sharp Shakespearean
sonnet-spewing quills.

Hawkish Apache's
beaded eagle crest.

Numeric Values

The Prime Mover
The Second Sex
The Third Wheel
The Four Seasons (see also Horseman)
The Fifth Dimension
The Sixth Sense
The Seven Hills (see also Dwarves)
The Eighth Wonder (see also Octomom)
The Nine Muses
The Tenth Inning
The Eleventh Hour
The Twelve Tribes

Cut to the Chase

Get a load of the gridlock on that one.
Somebody dumped sugar in her synthesizer.

Just thinking of it gives my brain a wedgie.
Seems like one thing is always in the process

of overtaking another even if they both move slower
than the decline of the Roman Empire.

Never was a person so hemmed in by the plaid-
striped-polka-dot pattern of thoughts.

The busier they are, the more doesn't happen.
Did you think of that all by yourself

while staring at the plasma-screen lake?
No, it's something I read in an old fortune cookie.

But it doesn't change the fact
that certain information is still missing.

I guess we could sit and wait.
Does anybody here remember how to dance?

Jaillight

Forgotten
          spice

on the tip
of my tongue.

The poverty
of poetry.

The poetry
of pouring in.

Yo y Tu

In Spanish
yo means I,

and *tu*
is a you
I know

or at least
am comfortable
addressing casually.

In English
we have no
informal form

to indicate
the you
still in pajamas —
hair wild,
drinking coffee.

Intimacy, friendship,
easy access —

in English
the informal you
is "Yo."

In Search of the Lost Diminutive

Suffix that croons
over objects like babies.

Caressing them.

Creating a verbal comfort zone —
shrinking all threats.

Dressing pets up
in doll clothes.

Serving demitasse cups
of dew —
                fairy food.

No monsters, adults,
or superpowers allowed.

Slight

A slight implies
if not an insult
(real or imagined)

at least something
unpleasant —

a slight cold,
a slight headache.

No one ever says:
"You make me slightly happy."

Although this, in fact,
is often the case.

Dear Martyr

Once I was like you,
so steady and able to see

one point — infinite
in all directions.

My senses sharp
like one who is
both hunter and prey,

weapon and prayer.

No other way home.

Let's Do Lunch

They share a table perched
high on stools,
two young women

in navy and beige
skirts and cardigans,
tan, bare legged,
earrings glistening.

The one with long, dark hair
appears on the verge
of tears. She rubs her hands

together and looks out
the window as if Sixth Ave
were a bleak battlefield
of continually dying men.

The other, with long, blonde hair,
leans forward, encouraging,
nodding often.

A luminous, perfectly red
apple rests on top of her phone
like a centerpiece in the middle
of the otherwise empty table.

Neither of them eats
or drinks a thing.

Shoulder to the Grindstone

Press your wing
into the morning's wax.

Make an impression.

Murmur and Motion

Always a rearrangement
of molecules

a girl in a top hat

a man in a red turban

three men studying scripture,
Bibles in hand.

Sparrows
and hexagons.

Bare chested
with well-oiled tattoos.

Are those cameras hidden in the trees
taking pictures of people taking pictures?

Yes, some guy with a tall Mohawk
is spitting on the flowers.

Dear Ovid

Divine
Lemon-lime
Aria

Giving modern love
A virile,
Roman air.

I do
Dig your
Olive aura —

Your glide
And glare.

Give me
Your urn

And I'll lend
You my lyre,

My mad money
Any old day.

Man, you *are*
A golden raven!

Damn, girl!
You're my gamine
On La via dell' Amore.

May I drive
Your demon?

Ride
Your river?

May I die
In your diner

Among red vinyl
And velour?

And live
Raving on
In your mural —

An angel
Or lemur?

Give me a nod
And voila —
I'm ready —

Really, I am.

Pathos

On the island of Pathos,
the gospel of pathos is written
by sad-eyed saints clutching bedraggled pets.

There one listens not to the sea,
but to the murmur of a thousand clichés
about the sea and to the perpetually sighing breeze.

Here is quite a thriving tourist industry,
with new people arriving daily wanting to see
the famous tableaus of suffering — the lovers' leap,
the spas that offer weeping cures.

O Pathos, not even Baudelaire
when he looked into the mirror of the old clown
was immune to your sunny charm.

A Story Begins

The same as other stories, but we follow along in case something different might happen.

Just one different thing. It leads us to a ledge and pushes us over.

Every story has a climax in a way life doesn't.

It puts us back where it found us. It opens our eyes, which weren't closed but felt that way because what we saw was happening inside the story.

We are the excess of the story — that which it cannot contain.

Washed ashore.

What was the story about?

I can't remember. A dwindling, dimwitted tribe.

Every month when the moon was full, they'd sacrifice another virgin but could never figure out why the crops still wouldn't grow.

Games of Medieval Sadness

1.

She visits a zoo
where clocks are caged,

and one hears the occasional
oceanic roar of time,

but more often it's the tickle
of quietly ticking breath.

Stupefied, the alarmist cuckoo
and towering grandfather giraffe

stare, unable to leave their century,
a moment reduced so small

they but vaguely remember
the wilds of infinity.

Life passes in what feels like a second since
each second can only be one lifetime long.

2.

You live in a castle of cake.

Your one possession,
your only weapon: a fork.

Clearly, you must eat the rich.

Swallow the decadent
ganache of their fantasies

while continually and assiduously
nursing the memory of a single bitter leaf.

3.

They have a dungeon
with my name on it.

When I wish to be chastised,
I need only log in

and enter the type of pain (physical,
psychological, shame, remorse, guilt)

along with the desired degree of intensity.
My password is “Please.”

My safe-word is “Wow — this is fun!”
My reminder question is “What is your favorite novel?”

My favorite novel is not *Crime and Punishment*.
My favorite novel is *Madame Bovary*.

Imbibing

A show globe
of red intensity,

a glass beacon
of medicinal yellow.

Both are only
colored water

meant to be drunk
with the eyes, and yet.

The ancients knew
that color heals,

makes a fine meal
for a ruined mind.

Things (maladies) thought
to go on forever

eventually do,
like summer, end.

A Blue Humming

sky

without the tall, thin,
striated wisps of cirrus-words

breaking up,

without the clotted cream
of cumulus-cloud porridge.

A practically thoughtless day
(opaque mind)

except for the palest hint
of gray on the horizon

suggesting a possible
reversal,

rehearsal of some still-distant
diffuse storm.

Vague apprehension
masquerading as a clear day.

A Date with an Undertaker

He liked to bathe, dress,
do their makeup himself.

Always brought flowers.
Made them sleep in a coffin.

Insisted on no talk
or movement during sex.

Only their eyes could flutter open
at the end when he gave the signal-kiss.

One young wanting-to-impress girl
worked hard at "playing dead"
by trying to "spiritualize" her thoughts.

But an older one said she took a special pride
in doing absolutely nothing and that this
was the kind of thing that couldn't be faked.

The Dizzy Staircase

No one was supposed to climb
its slinky cylinder of spirals
leading to an escape hatch in the sky.
The whole thing was just for show.
Why else would you plant a lighthouse
in the middle of a cemetery?
It was a nice touch of New England
stuck in the Midwest. Obviously
the work of an eccentric tycoon.
I remember blowing smoke rings
in the dim stairwell. How quickly
they'd vanish. We made it all the way
to the top a couple of times,
but there wasn't much to see.
Some trees — and the occasional stray
lost soul looking to be led out of darkness
by the faint beacon of our cigarettes.

Reznikoff's Clocks

I have a quarrel with the clock.
Quick, quick!
These inconsiderable seconds fill
the basins of our lives to overflowing,
and we are emptied
into the sink and pipes of death.
How furiously it ticks this fine morning.

~

. . . remembering clocks, the house-cats lapping time.

~

Our nightingale, the clock,
our lark
perched on the mantel
sings so steadily:
O bird of prey!

~

The clock
on the bookcase ticks,
the watch on the table ticks —
these busy insects
are eating away my world.

~

My hair was caught in the wheels of a clock
and torn from my head: see, now I am bald!

~

Now the plague of watches and of clocks nicks away
the day —
ten thousand thousand steps
tread upon the dawn;
ten thousand wheels
cross and criss-cross the day
and leave their ruts across its brightness;

the clocks
drip
in every room —
our lives are leaking from the places,
and the day's brightness dwindles into stars.

~

How pleasant
the silence of a holiday
to those who listen
to the long dialogue of heart and clock.

~

The clock strikes:
these are the steps of our departure.

~

Excuse me, sir,
are you Father Time?

Time Traveler's Potlatch

For Rousseau: A leopard of multi-colored spots.

For Edward Hopper: A perfect piece of lemon meringue pie in a diner at midnight, where the only other customer is Greta Garbo reading a book.

For John Cage: Seven empty birdcages, each corresponding to a musical note. Some are elaborate Victorian wicker affairs; some of simple bamboo.

For Nate Hawthorne: An electric train, a board game based on the Salem witch trials, and a bottle of fine sherry.

For T. S. Eliot: A crate of peaches with a note that reads: "I dare you."

For Laura Riding: A dictionary and a whip.

Higher Power

I dreamt you tall —

tall as Abe Lincoln
tall as a tall tale
tall as a tree in a green cashmere sweater.

You were kind, concerned,
but fatherly — far away.

The supple unicorn of your good looks
was lost in the forest, in the music of silent growth.

I shaded my eyes, looking earnestly up,
but the acorn of your face kept receding.

Distant Relatives

A dog's big, wet muzzle — milk-bone breath.

Does he ever think of me, who sat with him beneath the grown-up
table? Rolling a ball between us.

Dad says we can't afford to send a man to the moon this year,
but we can send a robot brother that's even better.

Just imagine his shiny body like a pie-plate reflector
beaming the kind of thing meant to inspire song.

But I found it sad to picture him there all alone,
jerking this way and that.

My father barking orders, telling him he'd better hurry
and finish cleaning up that huge, empty room.

The Honeycomb of Sleep

I sleep, you sleep, we all sleep.
In every cell,

we try to speak
but fall quickly

back to sleep
between sentences.

Throughout the hive,
one hears only

the busy signal of zzzzz's
doing their antiwork.

The Ones You Meet on the Way Up

The itsy bitsy spider I killed
returned to the exact same spot
on the wall in my dream. Only this time
much bigger and hairier. Louder too.
Its thin voice lashed out at me,
criss-crossing the room — instantaneously
capturing the pale crumb of my head
in its elaborate argument. It was speaking
High Spider, that ancient language
of clipped, grandiloquent tones.
My shoes were crazy-glued to the floor.
My cries to him were as doggerel.

Ode to Distraction

Give me something
not to pay attention to
and I'm happy.

Some things
grow better
with neglect —

spring up when the mind
is elsewhere.

A strange, wild flower
that doesn't care
for compliments.

It is also good to be lost
in some simple activity
you have no interest in.

Just as there is art for art's sake,
why not a pure form of distraction?

One says: "I love you to distraction,"
meaning, in a way, I can't stand
to actually see or think of you.

Repetition and Duration

Something lasts
as long as
it's repeated,

as long as
it's repeated as
long.

One works harder
at first
to make it
last,

noticing less and less
in the middle

until small differences
come out like stars.

The more often
it is said, thought, done,

the more
there
it becomes

solid
            transparent

an echo
not a voice

a given
not a choice.

The more there is,
the less we need to.

The Repairman

I can't get rid of him. One day I found him sprawled on the floor tinkering with the radiator. He was very vague about who had called him (not me) but seemed to think he had every right to be there. Then he handed me a bill for several thousand dollars. I said: "I can't deal with this now, I'm late for an appointment." But when I got to my office, he was already standing in the hallway, tapping the walls with a concerned look. "Structural tests," he said. After that I began seeing him everywhere, like a shadow carrying a toolbox. He followed me to school as sure as Mary's little lamb. Later, he followed me into a bar, sat a few stools away, sipped a beer, and made fun of my taste in game shows. He even had the audacity to ring my mother's doorbell on Thanksgiving, claiming he had come to look at the dishwasher but instead got into a discussion with her about fall fashions. In all fairness, he doesn't seem dangerous or malicious; he's never tried any funny business. But I have to ask myself if he's fixed one thing. The answer is I don't think he even tries. He just seems to want to be with me. Meanwhile, the bills keep coming.

Black Bag

A woman who wanted to change
dreamt the same dream every night

of losing her purse: lipstick, keys, ID.
Sometimes they were stolen,

sometimes she merely forgot them.
Every morning she'd check to see

if her purse was where she'd left it —
like looking into a mirror.

Sometimes she even knew in the middle
it was only a dream but still felt sad

as if she'd lost a dear friend.
In the bottomless black hole of the purse,

it seemed there was always a little more loss
left to lose — but maybe not,

which is why she'd always ask:
What if this time it's really gone?

Vanilla Orchids

Caught a whiff
of the blind woman's perfume

— something expensive —
as she left the restaurant.

Settled into the Oriental shawl
of her chair and closed my eyes.

Resolute —
to better sense
undiluted

those flowers
that only bloom in darkness.

Darkness Adds Beauty

To whatever
face or object
comes forward.

The nineteenth century is full
of haloed humble beings
flashing the sign of their presence.

In the twentieth century, only mystics
like Walter Benjamin would notice
and lament the loss of darkness

in a world overpopulated with things.
I remember one winter long ago
I saw an entire nativity scene

on the roof of a department store:
wise men, angels, sheep
lit up and peering down

into our small cold car,
reminding us to rejoice, and to buy,
and to rejoice in our buying.

Do You Think a Photocopy of a Snowflake Is More Beautiful than the Original?

for Joanna Fuhrman

Few know the gender of snow
or can tell at a glance the menacing design
at the storm-center of its crystalline mind.

But Williams, our dear doctor, speaks of
"the male snow which attacks and kills
silently as it falls muffling the world."

I'd like a meringue-crisp snow
under a thick blanket of synthetic bells.

I'd like a menagerie of snowflakes
running wild in a blank thicket
of wind tunnels and glass air.

Give someone a snowflake,
like one note from a symphony,
and what can it do?

But a photocopy of a snowflake
will hang forever in dazzling obscurity
above a bed.

Something's Coming

First Xmas, you gave me
Einstein's theory of relativity,
soap on a rope, *West Side Story*.

I gave you a bottle of Stolichnaya,
which you hated the taste of
(preferring the cheaper brand, Dimitri)
but you drank it anyway,
and it did make me happy.

In fact, the next day
a neighbor who helped us
dig my car out from under
a snowdrift said he'd never seen
two people so happy
to go to Burger King.

Varieties of Fire in Hilda Morley

under the snow a fire
barely moving

(as scallions are made
of electricity)

a spark of anguish

crackling:
            a live creature

the heart's fire
blown open
& set flying

voice . . .
sprung from the lion's mouth
by roots of fire

heat of the earth's
original honey

            All day
the pure heat
            blasts

the skin,
            the pores
golden,
            alit
with fire

moon-blaze

smoke-tears

fire of the eyes
looking

in the cold
fire of evening

fiery silence

the white flame
of a crystal brimming —
an edge of fire

Roman candles

(fireworks of conception)

the old stars returning
to their places

Three Unrelated

Bluebird gargoyles
menace with happiness.

~

Night

A hiccup
in the dark.

~

Alice, on Wonderland:

I've already tasted
all those things
marked "Eat Me"
and "Drink Me."

Restaurant Art

1.

Today's Special

Once still lifes hung above tables
offering food to gods before we ate.

They may also have served as signs —
a menu for those who couldn't read:
"I'll have the rabbit."

In dim rooms, baskets of painted flowers
bloom where real would prove too costly.

And for no extra charge,
paintings provide the illusion of music too —

the penetrating tune
of the Gypsy's eyes hovers
as he raises a fiddle to steaks and chops.

2.

The Upscale Sports Bar

strikes a balance
between raucous
and orderly;

the pillars
adorned with
faux graffiti

bring the lurid
urban scrawl inside,
domesticated,

while above the bar,
in place of honor,

three flat-screen TVS
like three-headed Cerberus
oversee the action.

3.

The Haunted Snack Shop

Everyday is yesterday
in the sepia-tinted air

beneath the blue neon smoke
rising from the red neon cup

as if Pound had declared:
"The diner is a poem containing history."

So I sit between photos
of Brooklyn Dodgers and guys
with impossibly wide lapels.

On back wall,
a Coca-Cola poster
depicts a globe with a giant hand

bursting from it,
raising a bottle of soda,
a frosty missile,

next to faded framed
front page proclaiming,
now as on D-Day:

INVASION BEGINS

4.

The Indie Café

White Italian lights
loop around
exposed pipes.

Brick wall, bare bones
low-budget chic.

Sloppy paintings
of sock puppets say:

"Fuck Art that tries."

Must be the work
of the inner child
of a friend of a friend.

A wobbly skyline melts
like hot fudge sauce
above a table in the corner.

Caught in a Downpour

If I open my mouth, I might drown.

Get In

The remedy
of his name
is fast acting.

In your blood,
you'll feel Ganesha
racing to reach you.

Thorn-locked places
melt to froth —
and blossom

as he crosses
one abyss
after another.

Pulls the limo
of his rat-drawn chariot
right up to your ledge.

Library of E

Black-and-green butterfly
Wedding-cake bride and groom
Robert Creeley
Barbara Guest

Joe B
Joe C

Jade elephant
Brass turtle
Red-and-white candy dice

Sappho
Lorine
Lorine
Lorine
Lorine

Tie-dye Easter eggs
Rimbaud bejeweled by David Shapiro

Pig and globe
Sarcophagus pencil box

The Futurist Cookbook
The Dead Celebrity Cookbook

Sei Shonagun
The Brothers Grimm

Library of J

Red Buddha
Silver rocket

Jack, Frank,
Stevens, Poe

Epics and matchbooks
Spirit money to burn

William James
John Dewey
Pierre Bourdieu

A photo of Elvis near
A photo of Mayakovsky's grave

Hegel
Marx
The Big Book
The Best of Mad

See iPad for more titles

Some

Some straightforward
                    yes and no

followed by
some circuitous.

Flimsy partitions
                    inserted.

New compartments created.

A repositioning
of the old line, as in
whose side are you on?

Some dead
                    and some living

remixed.

A shade too green
or purple.

Their faces
colored wrong.

Metallic

A gong is struck
in the temple of a dream,

signaling
          change.

On the bare stage
of a bare room,

some that are not there, come.
Others not there, go.

While we in the audience
assume new positions, ideas.

Like a spear, the sound travels
through the night

and next day — reverberates
still — a subtle difference

more felt than heard,
but distinctly.

Scrabble with the Illuminati

1.

Canary Radio

Mime
becomes
mimeo.

Snow
on the
zax box.

Voices
gel.

Have
becomes
shave.

Hew
becomes
whew.

Okra.
Ki.

Yes!

2.

Club Zig

Owner
axes
plans

for
banal
lemon

ants
advent
event.

3.

POOF!

Dad devoured the crone
and threw his fez
in the trash.

The djin
took out his pain kit.

The monk
took his dick in hand,

admonishing: "Don't be naïve.
It can't always be figs."

Blue Jay Way

for Vincent Katz

Like much great classic horror, it begins with fog. Fog and organ music.

A melodic, malevolent fog has settled upon sunny, sharp-edged L.A.

Everything is under the spell of its lostness, its slow-motion samsara.

Even the unseen birds contribute to the tangle with their winding, gliding ways.

The song itself is a spell inducing us to turn left when we should go right.

The singer's voice sounds distant and sleepy. Jet-lagged and drugged.

The singer-songwriter is George Harrison, who claims he was, in fact, jet-lagged when he wrote it while waiting for a friend late at night in a rented house on Blue Jay Way, a street high in the Hollywood Hills.

We listen as if to a hypnotist, and our eyes too begin to grow heavy.

We see ourselves from above — a bird's-eye view — driving the never-arriving car but also waiting back at the house.

After the droning intonation of each line comes a chorus of wraiths and banshees, wailing and rattling the chains of their distortion.

There is actually a backward version of the entire mix including vocals and all instruments faded up at the end of each phrase.

The song is spooky, but like most of George's compositions, it can also be spiritual.

The line "please don't be very long," repeated twenty-nine times, could be addressed to a casual friend, a lover, or to God.

I like the song not so much because it encourages me to keep looking, but because, thanks to its amazing technical wizardry, it perfectly replicates the muddled feeling of being lost.

Truth be told, as someone born during a Mercury retrograde, I rather like being lost. Even if you don't believe in astrology, I can assure you I have virtually no sense of direction, look at maps as a peculiar form of abstract art, and often find that places I've been to many times look totally unfamiliar. It's the exact opposite of déjà vu.

I like being lost for the same reason I used to like to smoke. It gives me an excuse, time to think, a way of being unaccountable, at least temporarily.

In our age of GPS systems and cell phones, it's hard to imagine a song like this being written. The whole situation seems quaint.

So why not succumb now and then, if only for nostalgia's sake, to the lure of the lost?

Tomorrow is sure to be business as usual.

Bardo Boulevard

A drowsy, bucolic nostalgia
for brewed wideness,
                                        neon cows.

A robot scarecrow
in a magnetic field.

Early morning
swarms of sunlight

creased   nattering

traffic in a maze.

C'mon, Really This Is Bullshit

Behind the sighing,
groaning, cursing,
shackles, hot stove,
backache, itch,
sky-high wall
of wanting to hide,
vodka waterfall,
I see him smiling
shyly, looking up
out of his tall body
as if he'd just told
an invisible joke,
whispered it telepathically,
and was waiting to see
if I would laugh.

Trees Rehearsing

tomorrow's
soft-spoken

over today's
sharp edge

The Courtyard

I call this an ashtray garden
or a handkerchief garden —

really just a small square
spread between two buildings

with a few flowers
embroidered on it.

Not big enough to have a picnic.

Maybe a cigarette
if smoking were permitted,
which it isn't.

Backward Glance

I live in a dormitory
of discontinued names:

Thelma, Irene, Estelle.

The combination of letters —
lost essence of another era.

Who were they?
What did they do?

They were Thelmas, Irenes, Estelles.

The Lives of Statues

"I love the smell of marble."—Julia Sinclair

Unblinking.

Statues like philosophers take their time.

Their thoughts span centuries
speaking
        a) volumes
        b) silence

speaking volumes of silence.

But not all are so serious.
Some statues love to go naked and wave swords.

Others require offerings of candy, liquor, perfume, smoke.

In parks, on buildings, in squares,
they oversee —

raise an arm that is missing a hand
in friendly greeting.

From statues, one can learn to pray
(why else are so many found in churches?)

and also to persevere
but not to wait —
that word isn't in their vocabulary.

Statues are born old.

Behind many great statues, an irate mother once stood saying:
"Don't do that or your face will freeze."

Mannequins being slaves to fashion
are not statues. They are temporal beings.

Statues select their own society.

The Egyptians had a ceremony,
"The Opening of the Mouth,"
for bringing statues and corpses to life.

The statues in Hindu temples are fanned
by devotees and entertained with music.

Lingams are bathed in honey and milk.

As Rodin's secretary, Rilke had to learn to take dictation from stones.

Lot's wife: she doesn't get a name; she doesn't even get to be a real statue. It's not fair!

On moonlit nights, how reassuring to discover
you're being followed by a statue.

Statues are nothing like ghosts.

Better Is Better than Not Better

Grateful today
for small things:

getting paid
        and paying bills,

my new orange
ring of Saturn
dinner plates,

        spaghetti,

wine,

the ability
to praise coherently
the books I love.

Happy Birthday, Doc!

Still subscribing
to your rain-
glazed theories.

The wheelbarrow,
a given —
we now turn

to the question
of what to feed
the chickens.

Resounding

after Zukofsky

I drink to you

only
with my ear's

chalice
of your voice.

Grand it is
to sing
as poets do

things both ordinary
and sublime —

weather, love,

a light-hearted lament
of days passing

in carefree, short-sleeved
sorrow.

Yes, grand
to look up
and see / hear

your words in the air,
sky's arcadia,

sharp and clear,
holding the high note
steady.

Zukofsky Revision

Upper limit thought
Lower limit noise

~

My thinking and logic
are by nature fuzzy.

If I wish to convey this accurately,
I must choose *not* the exact right word,

but rather the right inexact word
that allows for a similar amount
of vagueness and ambiguity.

~

New York is a noise Mecca
for horns, sirens, drills, shrieks,
whoops, harangues, and rants.

Here we are all Cage-y connoisseurs,
Calibans lulled by "a thousand twangling instruments"
and noisome airs.

~

It's hard to hear, rare to see a thought
present itself fully formed like Venus-
on-the-Half-Shell.

More often an arm or leg appears
caught in some sea monster's maw,

or just a stray word-shoe
floats above the waves.

Becomes

Becomes
        beckons
                beyond

even beyond.

The far
now nearly

becoming.

A Medium-Rare Serenade

Wed sun and rain,
mud and air,

moon and mirror.

Draw a window.
Squeeze a lemon.

Sow a square.

Do add more dew —
and a snore.

Men and women require dreams
as rooms require doors.

No drama? No, add some drama
but no remorse.

What about wealth?
To one add a dozen zeros.

Now, marinate wild onions and red rumors
in sweet liqueur.

Then simmer and stew
under a new nude rose dawn. Done.

Serial Seeing

A totality
claims to be,
but really —

how could it
contain everything?

Gaps
let the work
breathe,

let the reader
in among.

When art is
too complete,

you're locked outside

(a cold business)

with nothing left
to do but admire.

Literary Lipsticks

Red Wheelbarrow

I Have Eaten the Plums

Poppies in October

Pink Christmas

Red Weather

A Rose Is a Rose

Jaffa Juice

Watermelon Sugar

Frost at Midnight

Haiku Centos

for David Trinidad

1.

Because the known and the unknown touch.
I carry my clarity with me —
gallons of grape light.

2.

I complain like a flute.
Even suffering is made of air.
A sound has no legs to stand on.

3.

Odor of lines,
snow falling on the lemon trees
behind the inventor's garden.

Bill Brandt

One would never say
these photos could be anywhere.

The light is English light.

He showed plainly
the English quality of the air.

Like a miner's lamp,
his lens pierced the soot

to capture the alien landscape
of the body.

Impossibly white —
slope of shoulder, slab of thigh.

Whether fishmongers or maids,
Harold Pinter or Vanessa Redgrave,

his favorite subjects
are English and England.

One would never say
these photographs could be anywhere.

Phantom Anthem

I'll know my country
when I seize it —

like Columbus on the way
to someplace else —

and set my foot
upon its cloud.

O how solemn a business
is the relentless pursuit

of happiness as if it were
a fugitive from the law.

Now its flag is a teacup on an anvil;
now, a grasshopper on a field of stars.

But when I see the adorable children
of celebrities on playdates,

my joy is irrefutable —
only my denim is distressed.

And when I witness
how tenderly old and young

cradle their guns
and speak in the shadow

of ancient words like freedom.
Well, it never fails to bring a tear.

The Winner

He stood in the doorway looking moistly
into the distance: "When I receive my prize,
I know what sweater I'll be wearing.
I can see the smiles of family and friends,
some jealous, incredulous, some genuinely
happy for me — a stubborn, awkward child
finally grown luminous, handsome, strong.
And the wizened look of the old avant-garde
artist recognizing one of his own. Afterward,
there will be reggae music and pomegranate
martinis followed by marathon sessions
of the most amazing sex. O Prize — my Beloved —
true aphrodisiac! I will never give up my search
to find and hold you. Even if you turn out to be
nothing more than an index card on which
the word *prize* has been scrawled in magic marker
by an unsteady hand, even then I will believe
in your power. I will be what you say I am."

McCabe & Mrs. Miller

Altman painted the West
as if Renoir were thinking
of Hiroshige's tiny figures
crossing rope bridges in the snow.

He heard its lure as something between
a folk song sung by a Canadian
and an opium dream told in the accent
of a Cockney whore.

The movie is 98 percent atmosphere.
Lazy curls of smoke are always winding round
the frizzy hair everyone wore in the seventies —
Julie Christie and Shelley Duvall.
Both have amazingly long necks,
like the steeple of the town's one church
that catches fire.

All that's left of Warren Beatty is his hat.

Pegasus

How refreshing to ride
like a statue
          on horseback.

High but
          not too high,

nor enclosed.

Listening closely
to the landscape

through the animal's
sharp, inquisitive ears.

Muffin of Sunsets

The sky is melting. Me too.
Who hasn't seen it this way?

Pink between the castlework
of buildings.

Pensive syrup
drizzled over clouds.

It is almost catastrophic how heavenly.

A million poets, at least,
have stood in this very spot,
groceries in hand, wondering:

"Can I witness the Rapture
and still make it home in time for dinner?"

I Never Seem to Arrive

I do yoga
while watching TV

but then get interested
in what the guests
on talk shows are saying.

~

On the way
to anywhere,

I have to stop
at every café

for tiny cups of espresso
and blood orange sorbet.

~

Older self
to younger self:

"Foolish woman —

(sometimes I sound
all Old Testament)

Why do you burn
too much incense

and read too many poems?"

By the River of White Noise

Transfixed by the babble
of whispered water —

its hybrid language
of natural and artificial

sounds that could only flow
from the keyboard of a synthesizer.

Soothing because they put you
someplace impossible to locate.

Is it long ago or in the future?

I think I hear birds too,
somewhere in the mix
but not strident or chirpy.

Muted, they are either
very shy or very distant,
scattering the narcotic seeds
of subliminal songs
into the cooing calm.

Stationary Yet Adrift

Like a ship in a bottle
of moonlight. It's late.
The rain has stopped. Walking home
pleasantly buzzed.
Led by the nose through moist,
deciduous halls.
Led by the noise — yellow clang —
midnight sun of ginkgos
yellowing the street.
Literally turning it to gold.
The cars and pavement awash
in fan-shaped leaves.

Notes

"Dear Ovid" is an epithalamium for two poet friends of mine, Danny Rivera and Laura Modigliani. All the words in it are derived from recombinations of only the letters in both their names.

"Imbibing" mentions show globes, which are glass vessels containing a colorful liquid. Traditionally displayed in drugstores, they have been a symbol of pharmacy from seventeenth-century England to the early twentieth century in the US.

"Reznikoff's Clocks" is a cento comprised of my favorite lines about clocks and time in the work of Objectivist poet Charles Reznikoff.

"Time Traveler's Potlatch" was inspired by a Philip Lamantia poem of the same name. This form was, in fact, an actual game played by surrealist friends of his. The object is to offer extravagant gifts to artists, thinkers, inventors, and luminaries from other eras.

"Do You Think a Photocopy of a Snowflake Is More Beautiful than the Original?" is a line from a Joanna Fuhrman poem. She made a list of all the questions in her books and invited people to answer one or more of them in the form of a poem. This is the one I chose.

"Varieties of Fire in Hilda Morley" is a cento comprised of all my favorite lines of hers about fire.

"Happy Birthday, Doc!" was written to mark William Carlos Williams's birthday on September 17.

"Zukofsky Revision" is my corollary to LZ's famous statement "I'll tell you / About my *poetics* —/ music / speech / An integral /

Lower limit speech / Upper limit music." I wanted a more internal version and came up with: Poetry should take as its lower limit noise; upper limit, thought.

"A Medium-Rare Serenade" is an epithalamium for my niece, Marianne Elizabeth Equi and Aaron Matthew Andrews. As in "Dear Ovid," all the words are made from recombinations of only the letters in the bride and groom's names.

"Phantom Anthem" may be an unconscious appropriation of the title of one of Robert Grenier's wonderful books *(Phanton Anthems)*.

"Muffin of Sunsets" is a line taken from Joe Ceravolo's poem "Fits of Dawn."

FUNDER ACKNOWLEDGMENTS

Coffee House Press is an independent, nonprofit literary publisher. All of our books, including the one in your hands, are made possible through grants and gifts from foundations, corporate giving programs, state and federal support, and individuals that believe in the transformational power of literature.

This activity is made possible by the voters of Minnesota through a Minnesota State Arts Board Operating Support grant, thanks to a legislative appropriation from the arts and cultural heritage fund. We also receive major operating support from Amazon, the Bush Foundation, the McKnight Foundation, and Target. Our publishing program receives special project support from the Jerome Foundation and an award from the National Endowment for the Arts. To find out more about how NEA grants impact individuals and communities, visit www.arts.gov.

Coffee House Press receives additional support from many anonymous donors; the Alexander Family Fund; the Archer Bondarenko Munificence Fund; the Elmer L. & Eleanor J. Andersen Foundation; the David & Mary Anderson Family Foundation; the Patrick & Aimee Butler Family Foundation; the Buuck Family Foundation; the Carolyn Foundation; Dorsey & Whitney Foundation; Fredrikson & Byron, P.A.; the Lenfestey Family Foundation; the Mead Witter Foundation; the Schwab Charitable Fund; Schwegman, Lundberg & Woessner, P.A.; Penguin Group; the Private Client Reserve of US Bank; VSA Minnesota for the Metropolitan Regional Arts Council; the Archie D. & Bertha H. Walker Foundation; the Wells Fargo Foundation of Minnesota; and the Woessner Freeman Family Foundation.

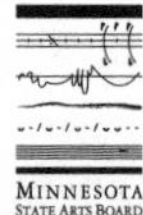

amazon.com

THE McKNIGHT FOUNDATION

THE PUBLISHER'S CIRCLE OF COFFEE HOUSE PRESS

Publisher's Circle members make significant contributions to Coffee House Press's annual giving campaign. Understanding that a strong financial base is necessary for the press to meet the challenges and opportunities that arise each year, this group plays a crucial part in the success of our mission.

"Coffee House Press believes that American literature should be as diverse as America itself. Known for consistently championing authors whose work challenges cultural and aesthetic norms, we believe their books deserve space in the marketplace of ideas. Publishing literature has never been an easy business, and publishing literature that truly takes risks is a cause we believe is worthy of significant support. We ask you to join us today in helping to ensure the future of Coffee House Press." —The Publisher's Circle Members of Coffee House Press

Publisher's Circle Members include: many anonymous donors, Mr. & Mrs. Rand L. Alexander, Suzanne Allen, Patricia Beithon, Bill Berkson & Connie Lewallen, Robert & Gail Buuck, Claire Casey, Louise Copeland, Jane Dalrymple-Hollo, Mary Ebert & Paul Stembler, Chris Fischbach & Katie Dublinski, Katharine Freeman, Sally French, Jocelyn Hale & Glenn Miller, Jeffrey Hom, Kenneth & Susan Kahn, Kenneth Koch Literary Estate, Stephen & Isabel Keating, Allan & Cinda Kornblum, Leslie Larson Maheras, Jim & Susan Lenfestey, Sarah Lutman & Rob Rudolph, Carol & Aaron Mack, George Mack, Joshua Mack, Gillian McCain, Mary & Malcolm McDermid, Sjur Midness & Briar Andresen, Peter Nelson & Jennifer Swenson, Marc Porter & James Hennessy, E. Thomas Binger & Rebecca Rand Fund of the Minneapolis Foundation, the Rehael Fund-Roger Hale & Nor Hall of the Minneapolis Foundation, Jeffrey Sugerman & Sarah Schultz, Nan Swid, Patricia Tilton, Stu Wilson & Melissa Barker, Warren D. Woessner & Iris C. Freeman, and Margaret & Angus Wurtele.

For more information about the Publisher's Circle and other ways to support Coffee House Press books, authors, and activities, please visit www.coffeehousepress.org/support or contact us at: info@coffeehousepress.org.

ALLAN KORNBLUM, 1949–2014

Vision is about looking at the world and seeing not what it is, but what it could be. Allan Kornblum's vision and leadership created Coffee House Press. To celebrate his legacy, every book we publish in 2015 will be in his memory.

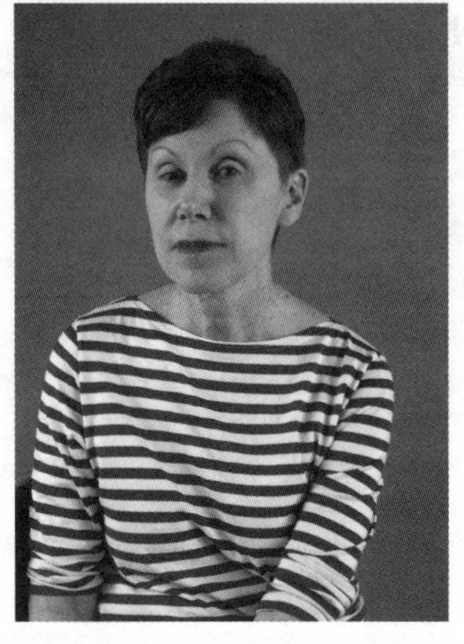

ELAINE EQUI was born in Oak Park, Illinois, and raised in Chicago and its outlying suburbs. In 1988, she moved to New York City with her husband, poet Jerome Sala. Over the years, her witty, aphoristic, and innovative work has become nationally and internationally known. Her book *Ripple Effect: New & Selected Poems* was a finalist for the Los Angeles Times Book Prize and on the shortlist for Canada's prestigious Griffin Poetry Prize.

Among her other titles are *Surface Tension, Decoy, Voice-Over,* which won the San Francisco State University Poetry Award, *The Cloud of Knowable Things,* and *Click and Clone.* Widely published and anthologized, her work has appeared in the *New Yorker, Poetry,* the *American Poetry Review,* the *Nation,* and numerous volumes of *The Best American Poetry.* She teaches at New York University and in the MFA program at The New School.